LOVING THOUGHTS

for

Loving Yourself
Health & Healing
Increasing Prosperity
A Perfect Day

~

Louise L. Hay

Eden Grove Editions

Texts of the Four Books of The "LOVING THOUGHTS" SERIES by
Louise L. Hay:

LOVING THOUGHTS FOR LOVING YOURSELF
LOVING THOUGHTS FOR HEALTH & HEALING
LOVING THOUGHTS FOR INCREASING PROSPERITY
LOVING THOUGHTS FOR A PERFECT DAY

Copyright © 1993 by Louise L. Hay

Original U.S. Publication 1993 by Hay House, Inc., Carson, California, U.S.A.

This edition published in Great Britain, 1996 by
Eden Grove Editions
8 The Arena
Mollison Avenue
Enfield
Middlesex EN3 7NJ

All rights reserved. No part of this book may be reproduced by any mechanical, photographic, or electronic process, or in the form of photographic recording, nor may it be stored in a retrieval system, transmitted, or otherwise be copied for public or private use – other than for "fair use" as brief quotations embodied in articles and reviews without prior written permission of the publisher.

ISBN 1 870845 15 3
A CIP catalogue record for this book is available from the British Library

Distributed in Great Britain by Airlift Book Company

Printed in Great Britain by The Guernsey Press Co. Ltd, Guernsey, Channel Islands

Introduction

The power of positive thinking is a well-known healing force even within the medical community. The positive, loving thoughts on the following pages are nothing more than positive affirmations.

You may feel that thinking a positive thought cannot possibly change your life, but how many times have you repeatedly affirmed a negative thought about yourself until finally it became true for you? Why not change those negative thoughts to positive ones?

I like to compare positive affirmations to planting a seed. You don't just plant the seed and get a beautiful flower the next day. It takes time. First you must water and nurture the seed and make sure it is safe from harm. It is the same with positive affirmations. You may not see changes immediately, but with enough nurturing and encouragement you can change your old negative way of thinking and look at things in a new and positive light.

Use these affirmations daily and over time you will begin to see your life turn in new directions and you will reap a bountiful harvest of positive, loving endeavours for yourself.

All is well,

Louise L. Hay

CONTENTS

Loving Thoughts

for

Loving Yourself . . . . page 7

Health & Healing . . . . page 69

Increasing Prosperity . . page 131

A Perfect Day . . . . . page 193

Loving Thoughts

for

Loving Yourself

Today...

the love in my world is a mirror of the love within me.

Today...

*loving relationships
begin with me.*

Today...

I love and cherish myself.

Today...

I open my heart to myself.

Today...

I love myself a little bit more.

Today...

love works miracles in my life.

Today...

love is the most powerful healing force I know.

Today...

forgiveness has opened the doorway to my own love.

Today...

*I help to create
a world where
it is safe to love
each other.*

Today...

*the more love I give,
the more love
I receive.*

Today...

*and every day
loving gets easier.*

Today...

*events may come
and go.
but the love for
myself is constant
and true.*

Today...

I dedicate this day to loving myself more.

Today...

*wherever I go
and whoever I meet,
I always find love
waiting for me.*

Today...

somewhere someone is looking for exactly what I have to offer.

Today...

I attract more loving relationships into my life as I relax and accept myself exactly as I am.

Today...

it is safe to let the love in.

Today...

love is my divine right.

Today...

I have lots of friends who love me.

Today...

*when I really
love myself,
everything in my
life works.*

Today...

*I give myself
the gift of
unconditional love.*

Today...

*the more love I give
the more I have
to give.*

Today...

when I look into a mirror it is easy for me to say, "I love you. I really love you."

Today...

*there is
an endless well
of love within me
and I share it with
others.*

Today...

I am worthy of love.

Today...

*loving myself
and others
gets easier.*

Today...

*I bless my parents
with love
and release them to
happiness that is
meaningful to them.*

Today...

I have a harmonious, loving relationship with all my family.

Today...

*by sharing love
we can all live in
peace.*

Today...

*all is well
in my loving world.*

Loving Thoughts for Health & Healing

Today...

I choose to be happy, healthy and whole.

Today...

*is the time
for healing.*

Today...

*I listen with love
to my own
body's messages.*

Today...

my body, mind, and spirit are a healthy team.

Today...

my body is a glorious place to live.

Today...

*I open my heart
and allow
my healing gifts
to flow.*

Today...

*every cell
in my body responds
to every thought
I think. therefore
I think positive.
peace-filled loving
thoughts.*

Today...

*I remember
to breathe deeply
and to fully relax
my body and mind
often during
the day.*

Today...

*I allow the love
from my own heart
to wash through me
and cleanse and heal
every part of my
body and emotions.*

Today...

and every day my body's natural desire is to be healthy, whole and complete.

Today...

I feel glorious, dynamic energy within me.

Today...

*and very day
my health is getting
better all the time.*

Today...

*my mind and body are in perfect balance.
I am healthy and harmonious.*

Today...

I recognize my body as a wondrous and magnificent machine, and I feel privileged to live in it.

Today...

*I inhale
the precious breath
of life, and I allow
my body, my mind,
and my emotions
to relax.*

Today...

*I look terrific
and
I feel terrific.*

Today...

*it gives me joy
to take loving care
of myself.*

Today...

*I approve of
my body exactly
as it is.*

Today...

I am grateful for my perfect, vibrant, radiant health.

Today...

strength and wholeness return to my body.

Today...

*I listen to
my body and
lovingly respond to
its needs.*

Today...

*I know
I am worth
healing.*

Today...

I have a wonderful, loving relationship with my health practitioner.

Today...

through self-acceptance I move into wholeness and health.

Today...

*every cell
in my body
responds positively
to my positive
mental images.*

Today...

*vibrant health
is my constant
companion.*

Today...

*I bring into my life
every person,
place and thing
I need for my
complete healing.*

Today...

my body knows how to be healthy.

Today...

every organ, muscle, joint and cell in my body is loved and appreciated.

Today...

*all is well
in my healthy
world.*

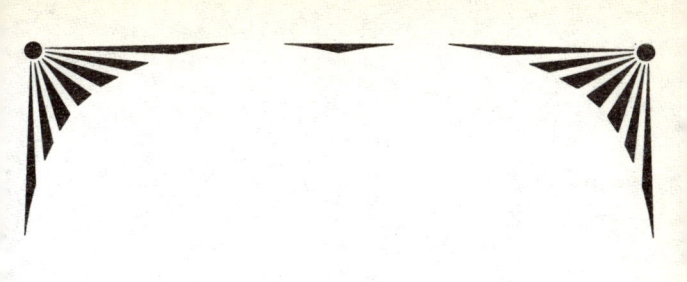

Loving Thoughts for Increasing Prosperity

Today...

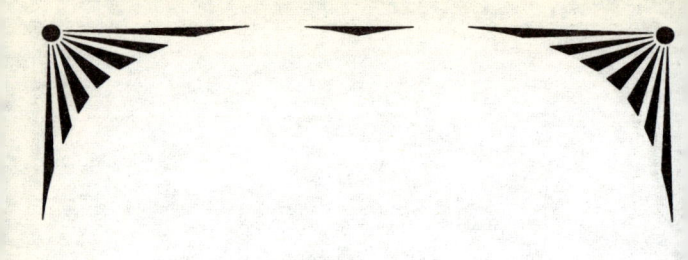

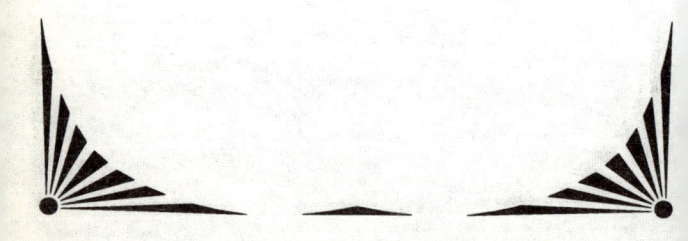

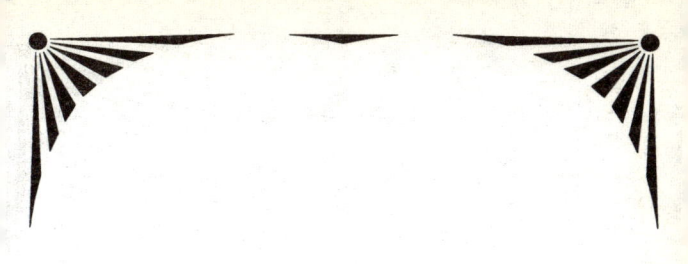

I choose to attract prosperity.

Today...

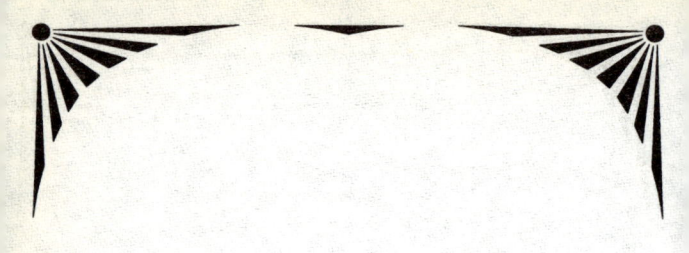

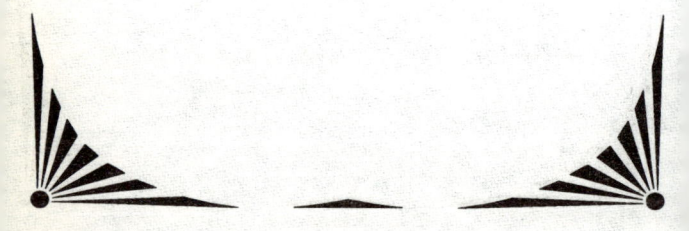

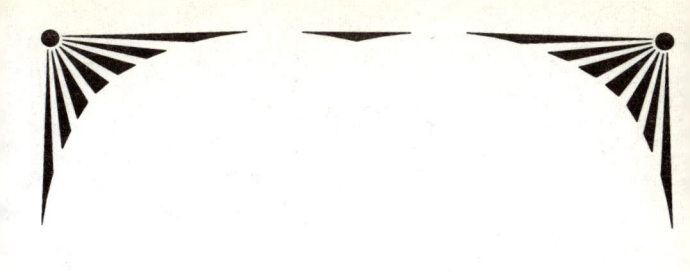

I accept a life filled with rewards and fulfillment.

Today...

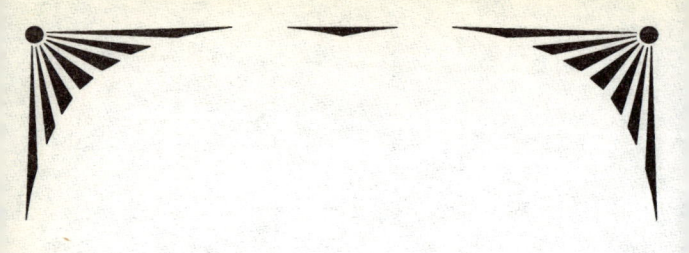

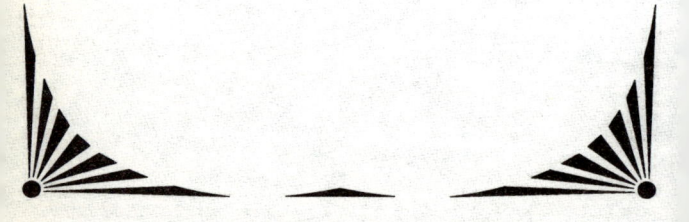

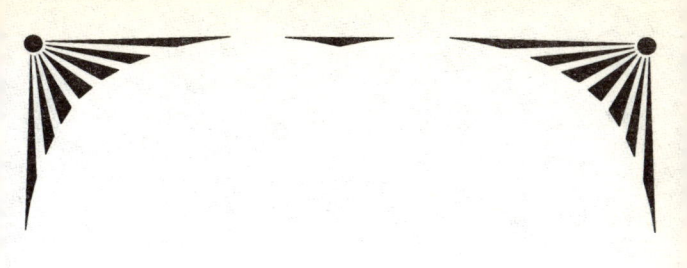

everything I touch is a success.

Today...

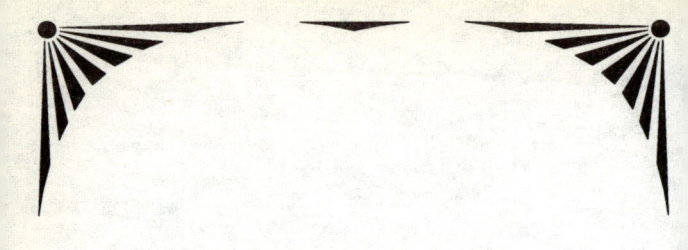

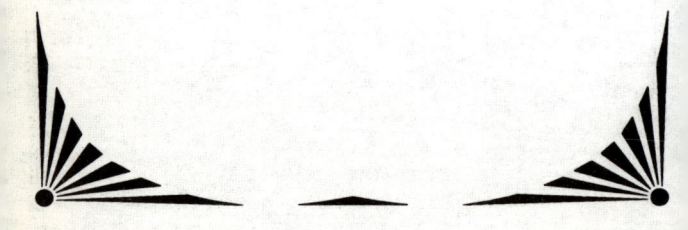

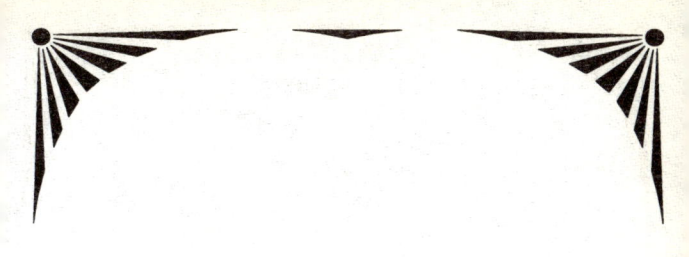

I know how to accept gifts graciously with a simple "thank you."

Today...

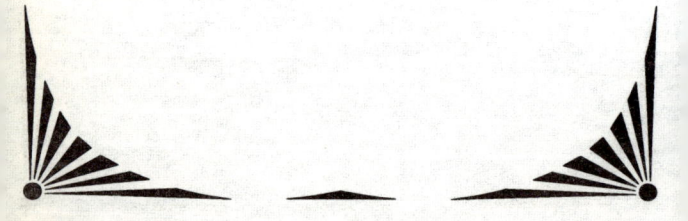

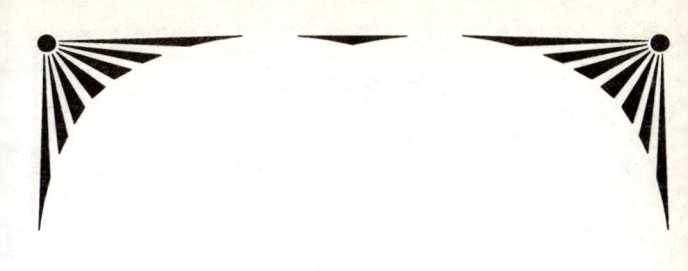

I create a good life for myself because I deserve.

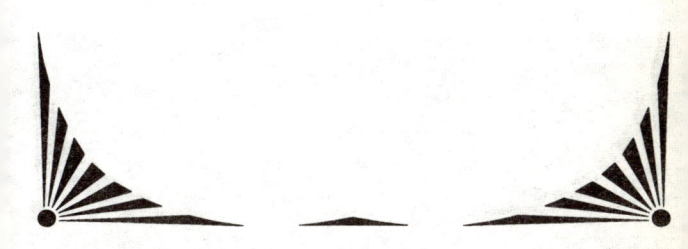

Today...

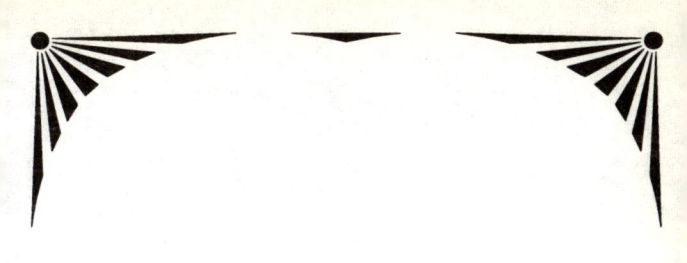

*I allow prosperity
to enter my life
on a new level.*

Today...

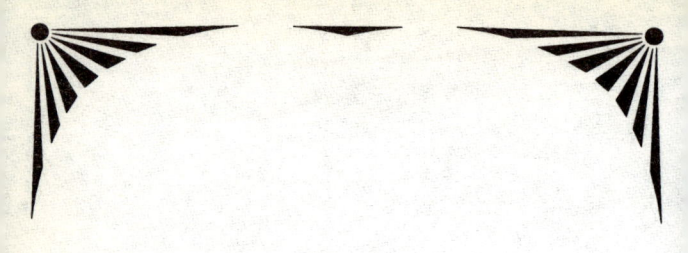

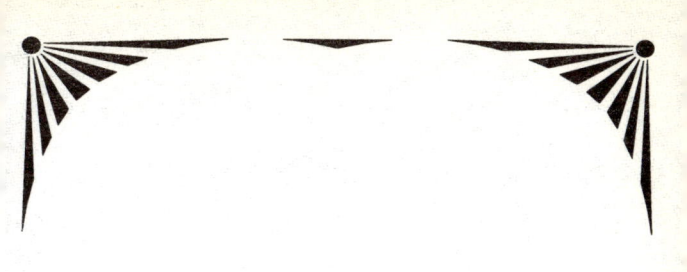

I rejoice in life's abundance and appreciate all that I have.

Today...

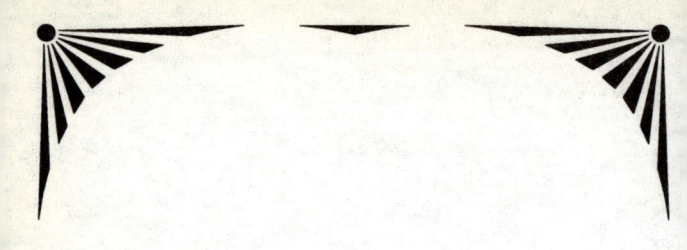

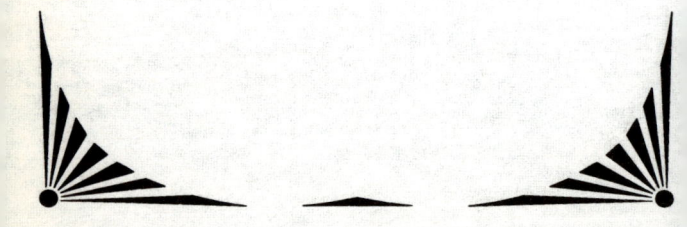

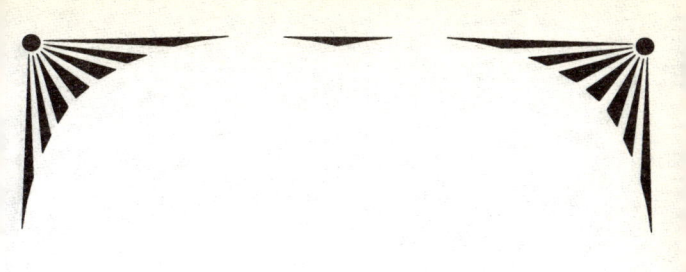

*I trust life
to supply me with
everything I need.*

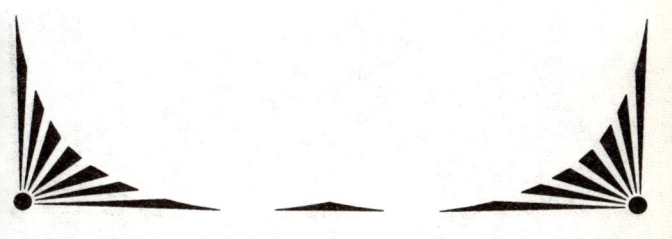

Today...

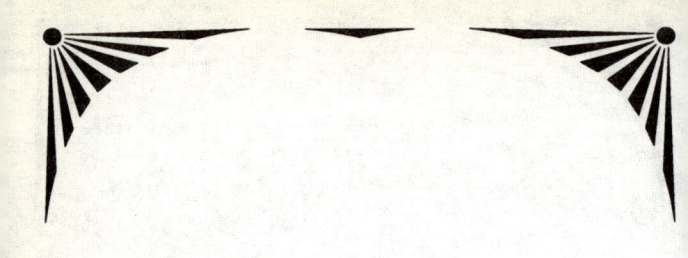

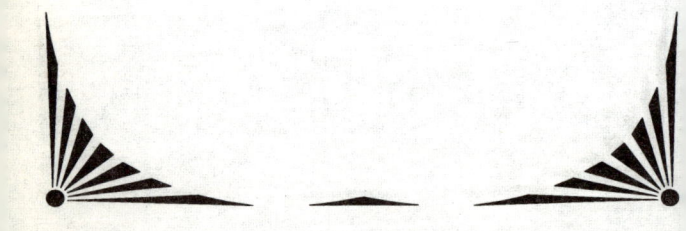

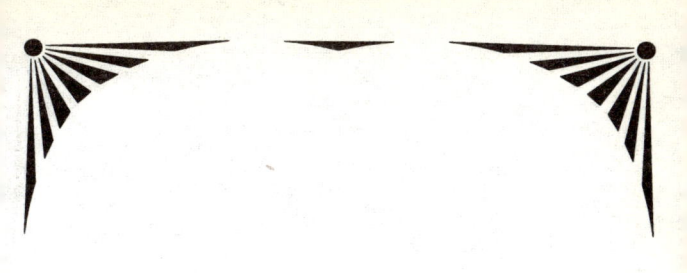

unexpected good is coming my way from unexpected sources.

Today...

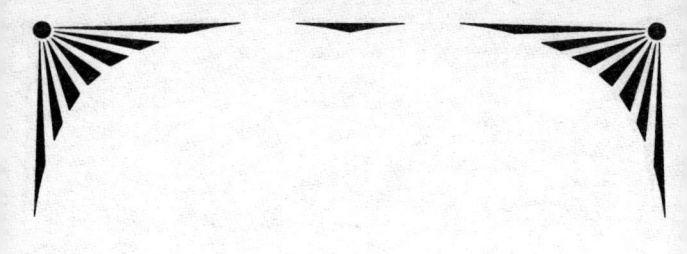

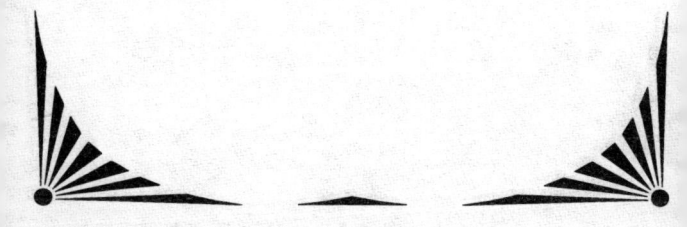

all my needs and desires are met before I even ask.

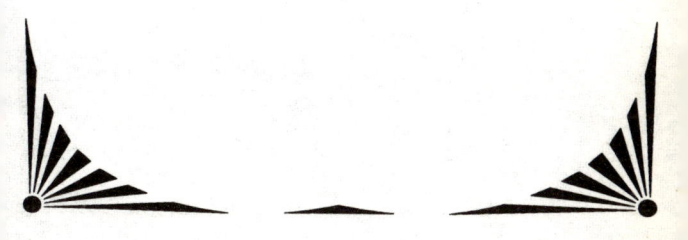

Today...

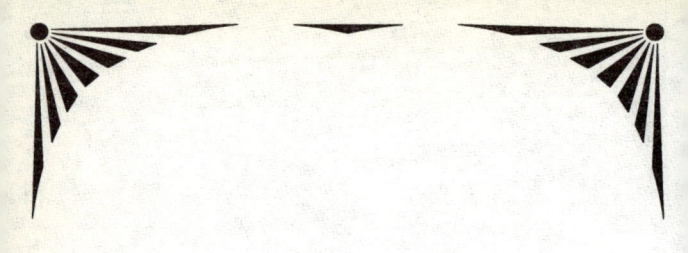

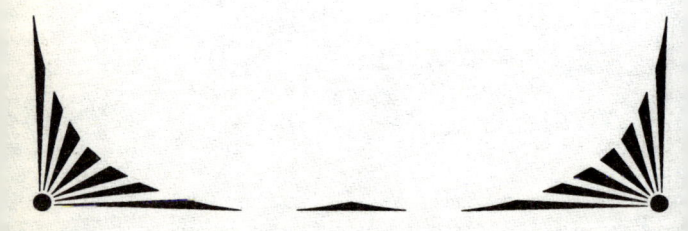

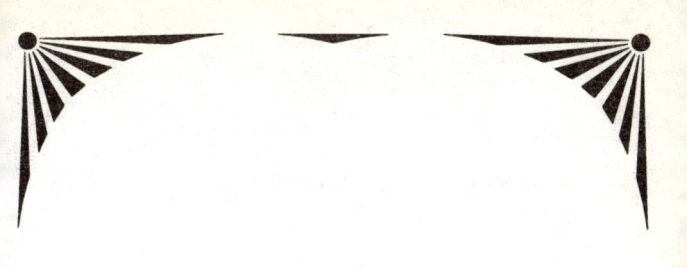

I allow my income to constantly expand.

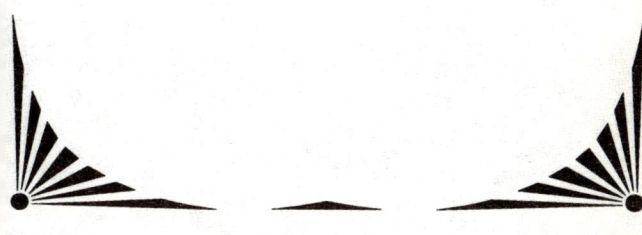

Today...

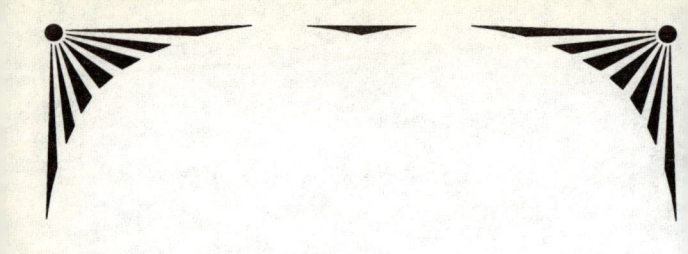

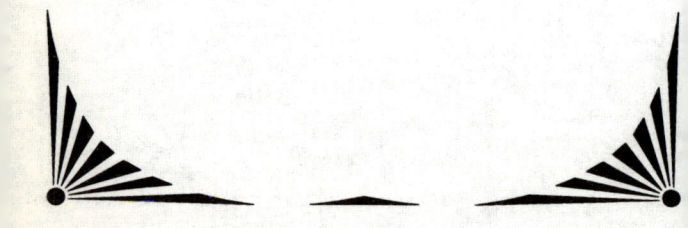

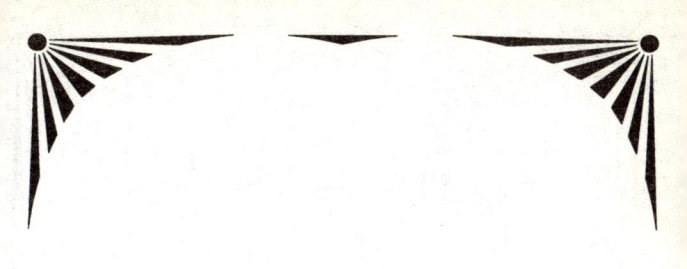

*I allow myself to
receive abundance
from the
Ocean of Life.*

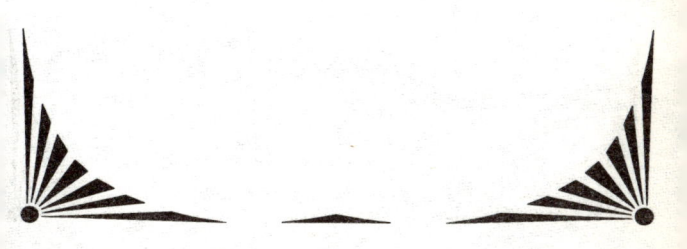

Today...

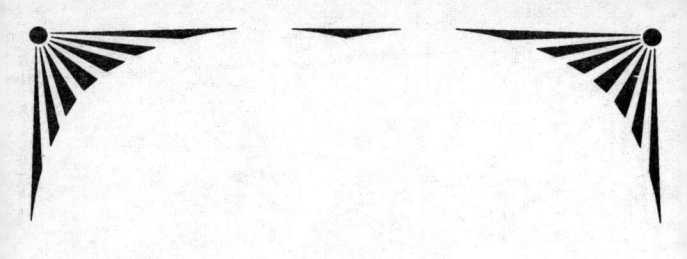

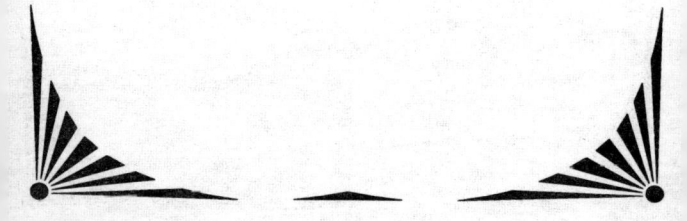

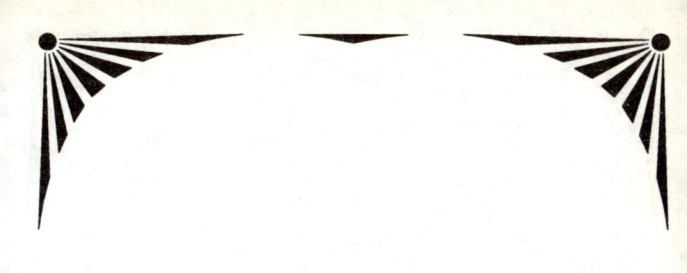

life knows my needs and generously supplies them all.

Today...

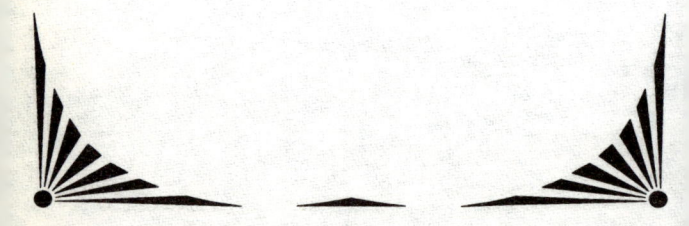

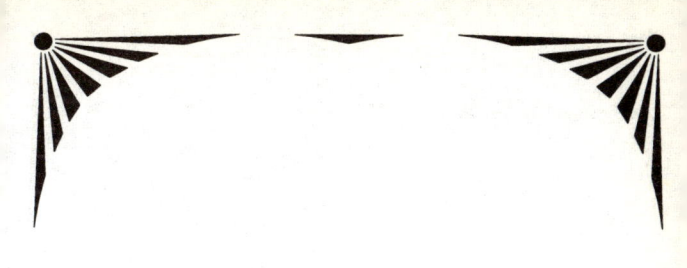

it is my birthright to share in the abundance and prosperity of this world.

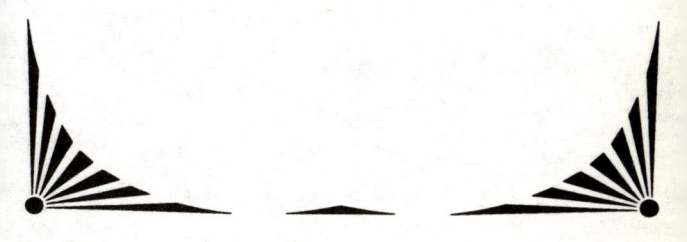

Today...

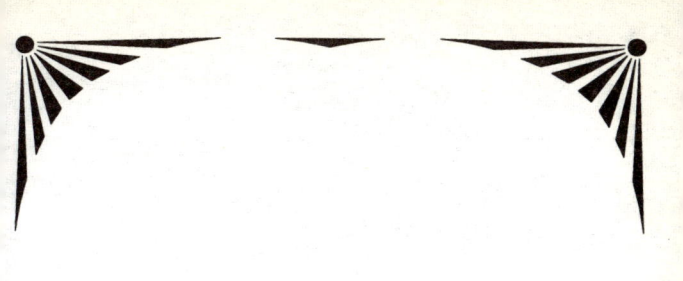

I am unlimited in my wealth.

Today...

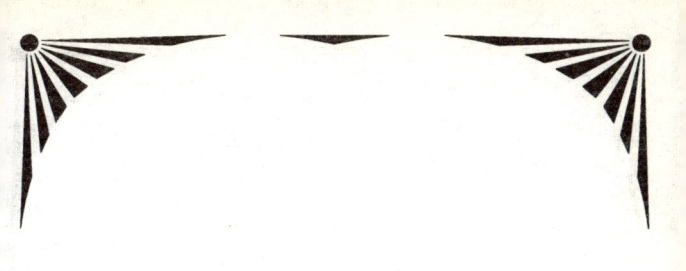

I am open and receptive to new avenues of income.

Today...

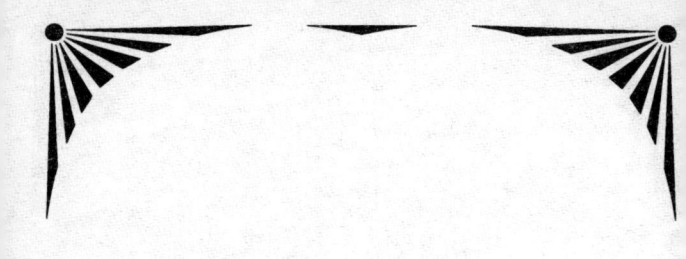

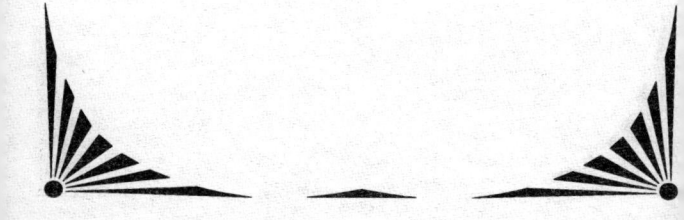

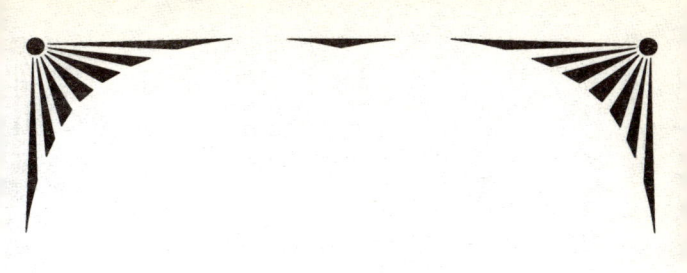

my good comes from everywhere and everyone and everything.

Today...

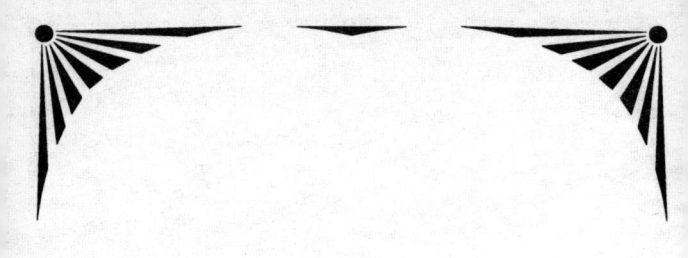

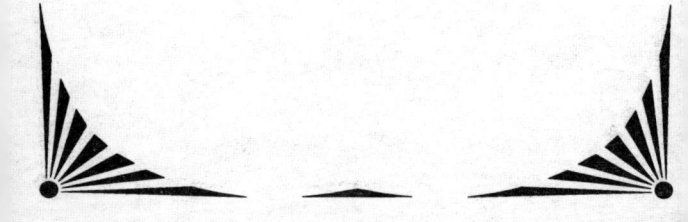

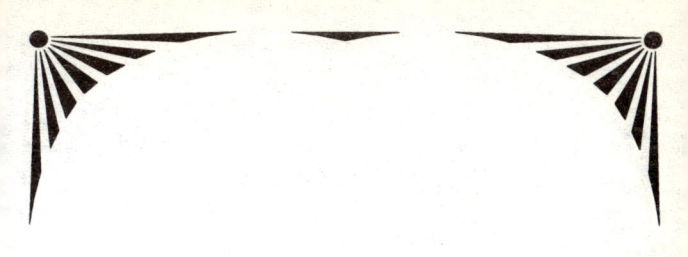

I give myself permission to be all that I can be and to deserve the very best in life.

Today...

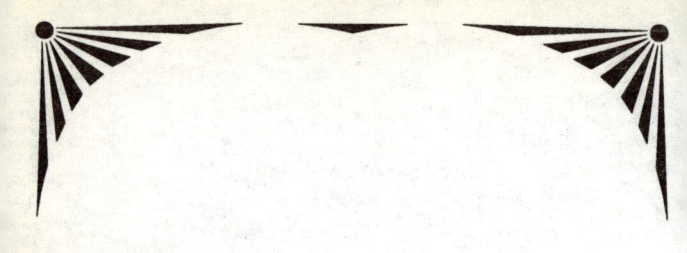

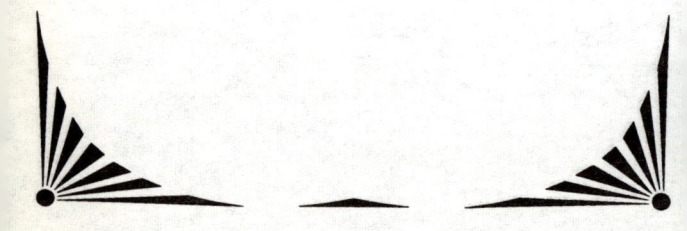

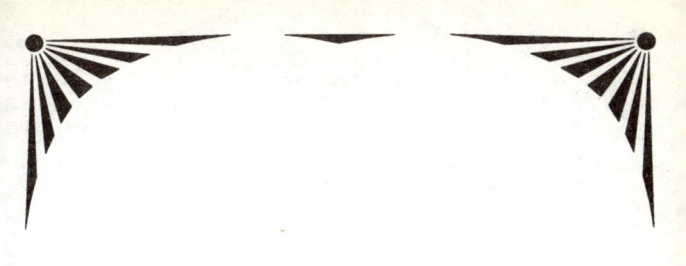

*I am totally
and completely
supported by the
Universe.*

Today...

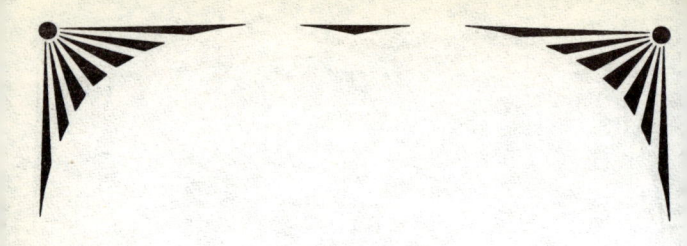

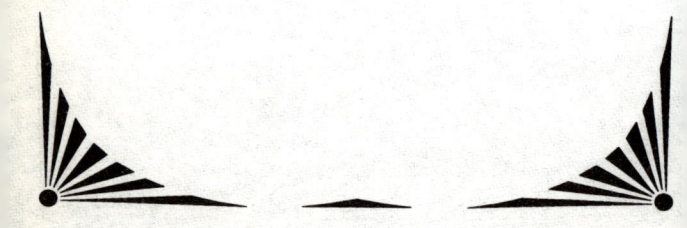

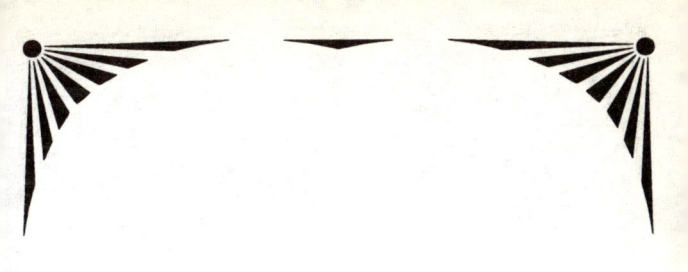

I accept with joy and pleasure all the good life offers me.

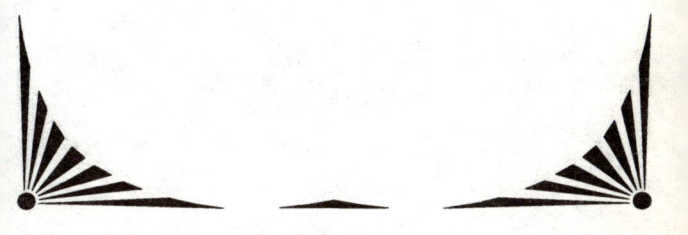

Today...

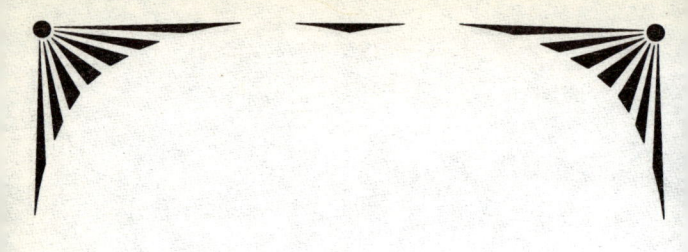

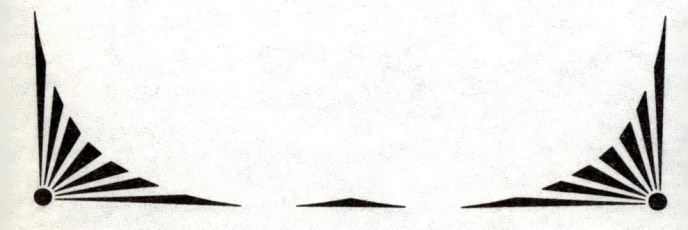

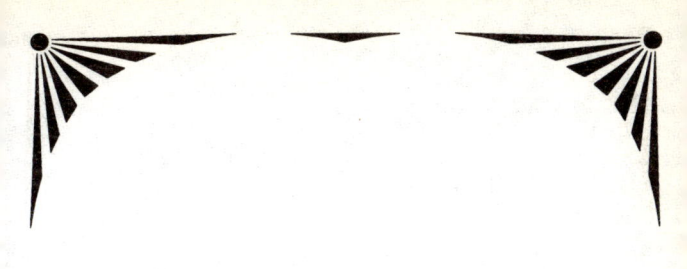

my prosperous thoughts create my prosperous world.

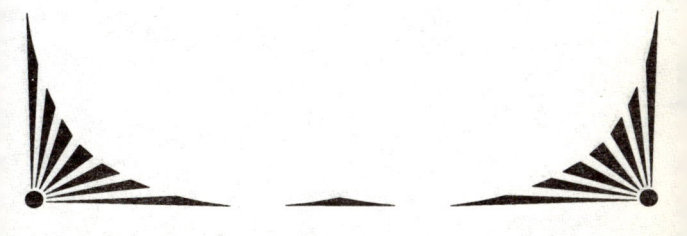

Today...

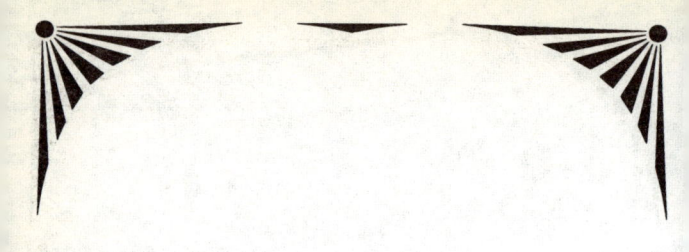

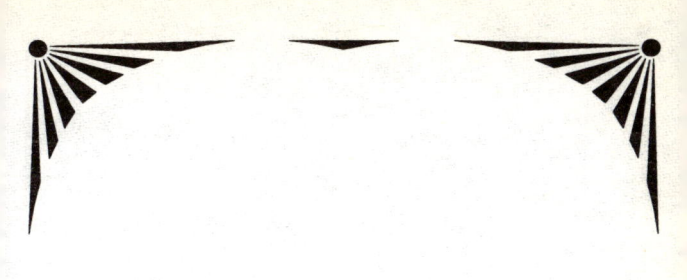

I release all belief in lack and limitation.

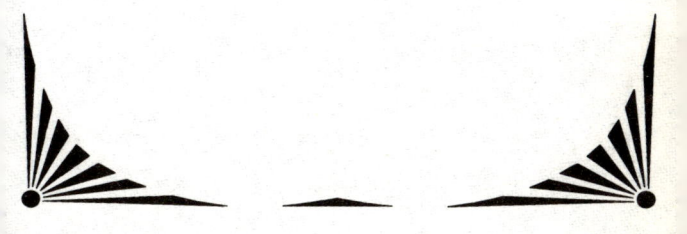

Today...

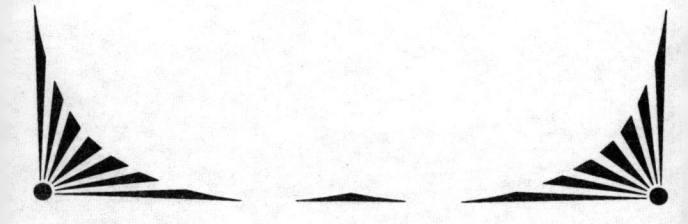

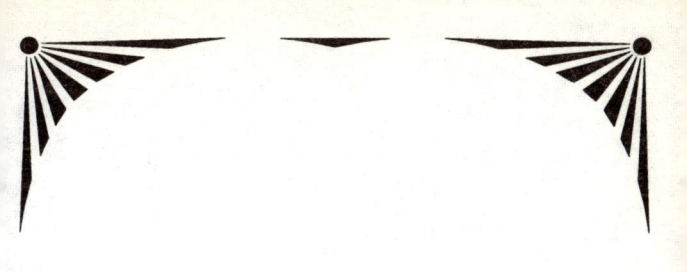

*begins a new era
of prosperity
and security.*

Today...

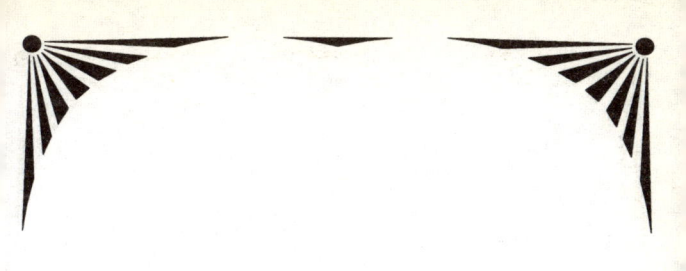

I give myself permission to prosper.

Today...

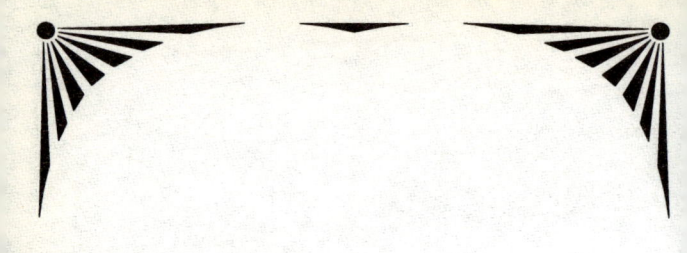

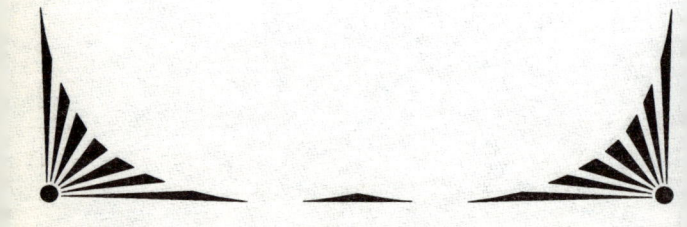

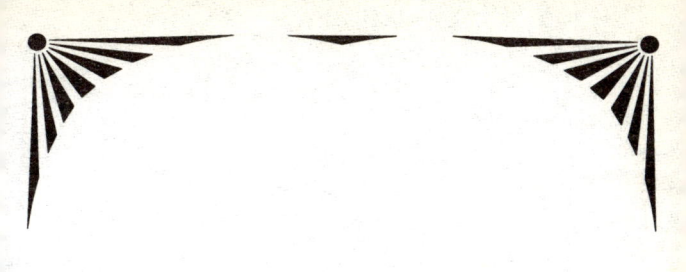

I bless my bills with love and pay them with joy.

Today...

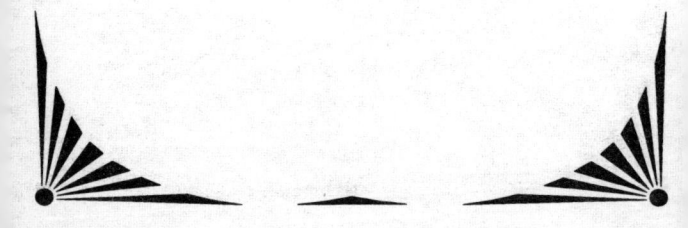

I am safe and secure and financially solvent.

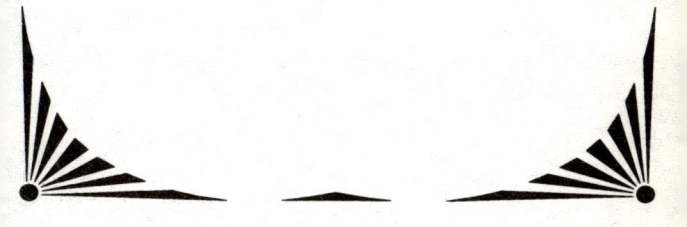

Today...

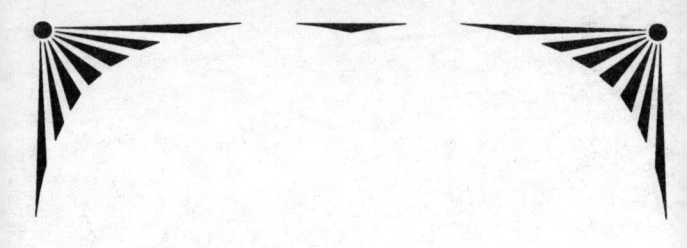

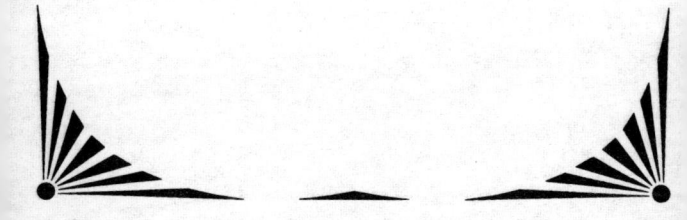

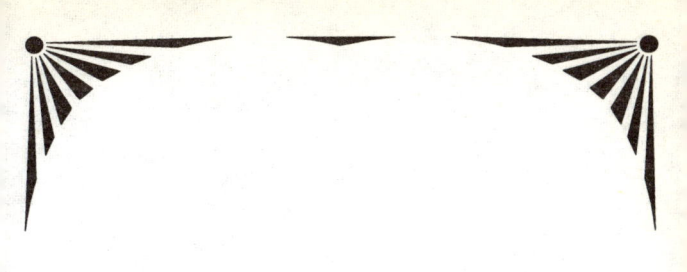

I give thanks for all good and all supply.

Today...

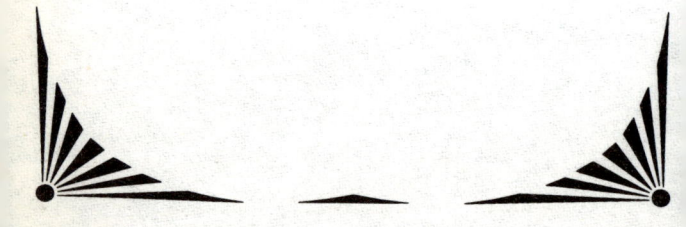

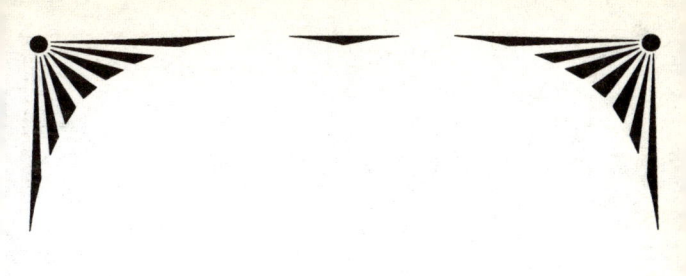

new doors are opening.

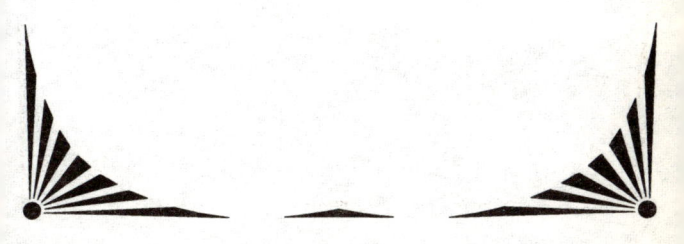

Today...

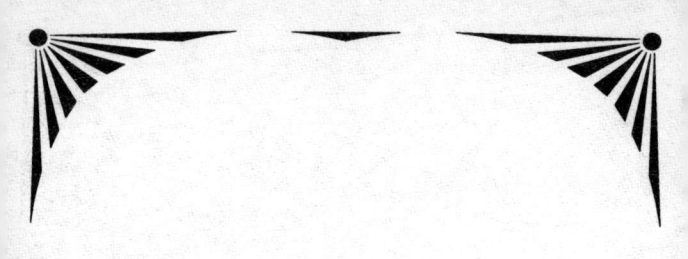

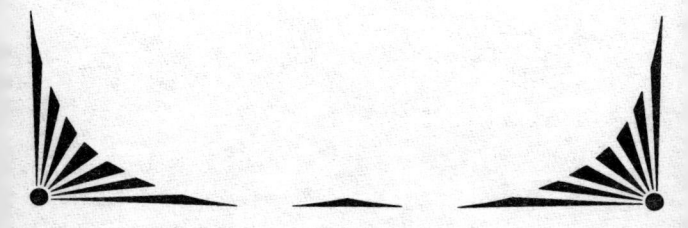

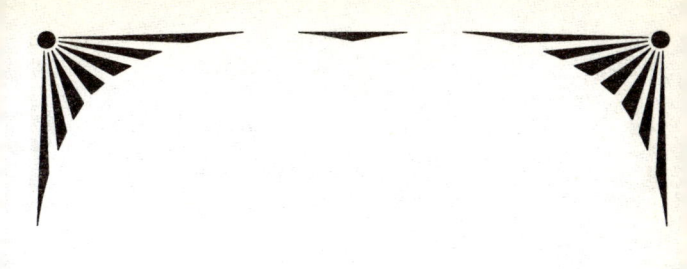

my life is filled with an abundance of all good.

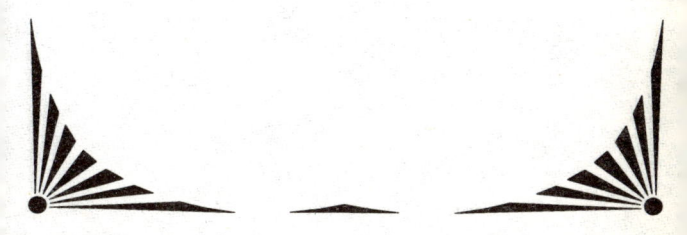

Today...

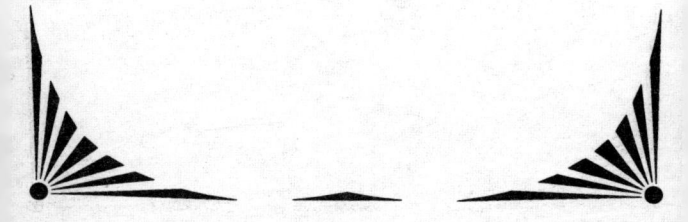

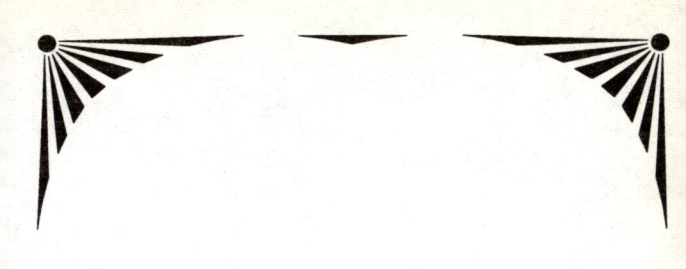

*all is well
in my prosperous
world.*

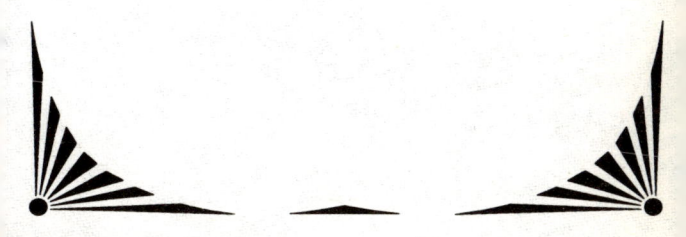

Loving Thoughts for A Perfect Day

Today...

*begins with
gratitude and joy.*

Today...

*I open a
new door of
understanding.*

Today...

*I am willing
to let go of all
negative beliefs and
to allow my own
deeper wisdom to
reveal itself to me.*

Today...

I am eager to expand my understanding and wisdom.

Today...

*there is more
for me to learn
each day.*

Today...

I choose thoughts that support and nourish me.

Today...

I am secure with being myself in all situations.

Today...

*I relax knowing
I am in
the right place at
the right time doing
the right thing.*

Today...

*all the wisdom
of the universe
is available to me.*

Today...

all my needs are met and all my questions are answered.

Today...

I draw easily upon intelligence, courage and self-worth for they are always with me.

Today...

I am strongly centred in wisdom and truth.

Today...

I know that everything in my life happens in the perfect time/space sequence.

Today...

*I open a new door
to self-esteem
and self-worth.*

Today...

my life is getting better.

Today...

*I lovingly accept
my decisions,
knowing I am
always free
to change.*

Today...

I move forward with confidence and ease.

Today...

*I rely on
Divine Wisdom
and Guidance
to protect me.*

Today...

*when I listen
to my inner self
I hear the answers
I need.*

Today...

*I see within myself
a magnificent being,
wise and beautiful.*

Today...

*whatever I need
to know is
revealed to me.*

Today...

I release the need to blame anyone, including myself.

Today...

*I am guided
in making right
choices.*

Today...

habits and beliefs that are no longer for my highest good fall away from me.

Today...

life supports me and brings me only good and positive experiences.

Today...

*I am discovering
how strong and
powerful and
incredibly capable
I am.*

Today...

I find the power within myself to make positive changes.

Today...

*my self-esteem
is increasing.*

Today...

I know life is for me and I joyfully look forward to the future.

Today...

all is well in my loving world.

BOOKS, AUDIOS & VIDEOS BY
Louise L. Hay

BOOKS

The Aids Book: Creating a Positive Approach
Colors & Numbers
A Garden of Thoughts: My Affirmation Journal
Heal Your Body
Heart Thoughts: A Treasury of Inner Wisdom
Life: Reflections on Your Journey
Loving Thoughts for Loving Yourself, Health & Healing,
Increasing Prosperity, A Perfect Day
Love Your Body
Love Yourself, Heal Your Life Workbook
Meditations to Heal Your Life
101 Power Thoughts
The Power is Within You
You Can Heal Your Life

AUDIO CASSETTES

Aids: A Positive Approach
Cancer: Discovering Your Healing Power
Empowering Women
Feeling Fine Affirmations
Gift of the Present with Joshua Leeds

Heal Your Body (Book-on-Tape)
Life! - Reflections On Your Journey (Book-on-Tape)
Love Your Body (Book-on-Tape)
Loving Yourself
Meditations for Personal Healing
Morning and Evening Meditations
101 Power Thoughts
Overcoming Fears
The Power is Within You (Book-on-Tape)
The Power is Within You (Abridged Book-on-Tape)
Self Healing
Songs of Affirmation with Joshua Leeds
What I Believe/Deep Relaxation
You Can Heal Your Life Study Course
You Can Heal Your Life (Book-on-Tape)
You Can Heal Your Life (Abridged Book-on-Tape)

Conversations on Living Lecture Series

Change and Transition
Dissolving Barriers
The Forgotten Child Within
How to Love Yourself
The Power of Your Spoken Word
Receiving Prosperity

Totality of Possibilities
Your Thoughts Create Your Life

Personal Power Through Imagery Series

Anger Releasing
Forgiveness/Loving the Inner Child

Subliminal Mastery Series

Feeling Fine Affirmations
Love Your Body Affirmations
Safe Driving Affirmations
Self-Esteem Affirmations
Self-Healing Affirmations
Stress-Free Affirmations

VIDEO CASSETTES

Dissolving Barriers*
Doors Opening: A Positive Approach to Aids*
Receiving Prosperity*
You Can Heal Your Life Study Course
Your Thoughts Create Your Life*

* N.T.S.C. VHS format only